Volcano breaks through the sea   4 An island is born

de view
— Volcanic island
— Coral growth

— Coral colony
— Channel widens
— Island sinks

— Coral atoll
— Shallow lagoon
— Island now sunk

3

4

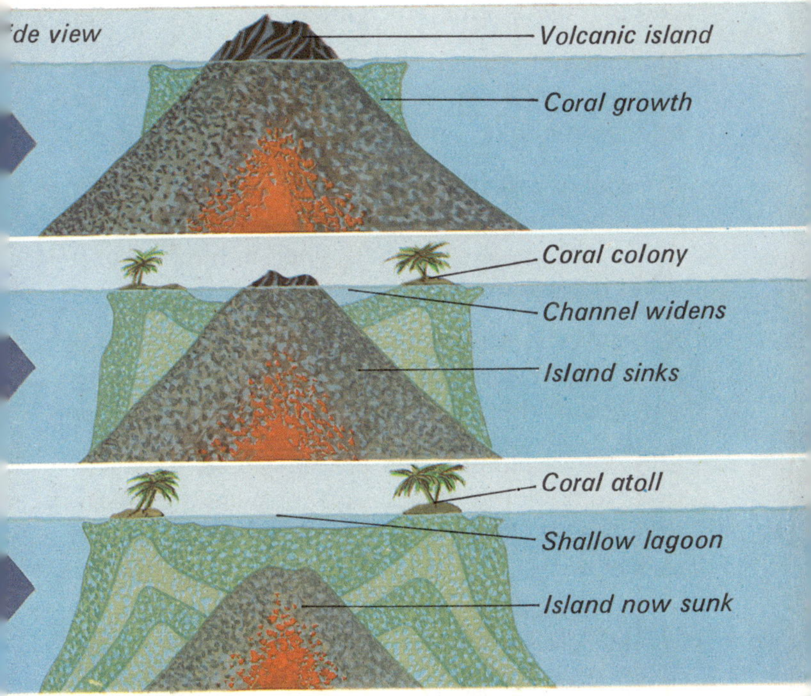

to teachers and parents

This is a LADYBIRD LEADER book, one of a series specially produced to meet the very real need for carefully planned *first information books* that instantly attract enquiring minds and stimulate reluctant readers.

The subject matter and vocabulary have been selected with expert assistance, and the brief and simple text is printed in large, clear type.

Children's questions are anticipated and facts presented in a logical sequence. Where possible, the books show what happened in the past and what is relevant today.

Special artwork has been commissioned to set a standard rarely seen in books for this reading age and at this price.

Full colour illustrations are on all 48 pages to give maximum impact and provide the extra enrichment that is the aim of all Ladybird Leaders.

Acknowledgment

The publishers wish to acknowledge the help given by Mr Hugh Brown, Warden at Beinn Eighe Reserve, in providing reference photographs for the illustrations on pages 20-21, and Cable and Wireless Ltd for reference material for page 39.

© LADYBIRD BOOKS LTD MCMLXXIX

All rights reserved. No part of this publication may be reproduced, stored in a retrieval system, or transmitted in any form or by any means, electronic, mechanical, photo-copying, recording or otherwise, without the prior consent of the copyright owner.

A Ladybird Leader
islands

by Patrick Armstrong, BSc MA PhD
with illustrations by
Gerald Witcomb, MSIAD

Ladybird Books Loughborough

Islands

An island is a piece of land with water all round it.
Greenland and Australia are very large islands.

In the Pacific Ocean there are thousands of tiny islands.

How some islands form

Some islands are really parts
of nearby large land masses
that have been cut off
by a rise in sea level.
Long ago Britain was probably
part of the continent of Europe
and Ireland was joined to Britain.

Volcanic islands

Other islands have been formed
by volcanoes growing up
from the bottom of the sea.

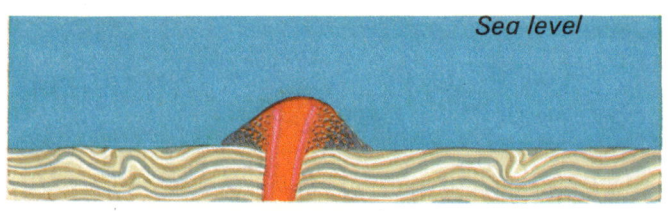

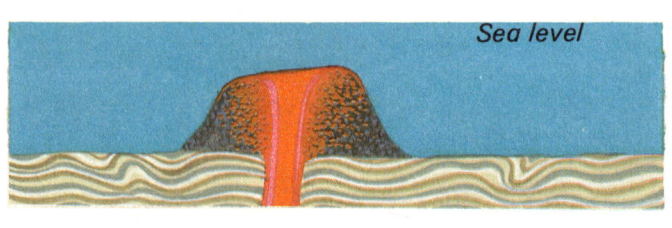

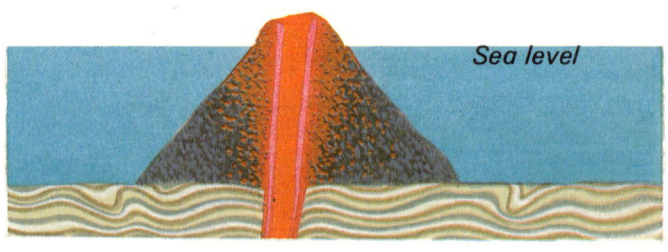

Molten rock or *lava*
comes out of the sea-bed.
It turns into solid rock
as it reaches the cold water.
The Hawaiian islands formed
in this way over millions of years.

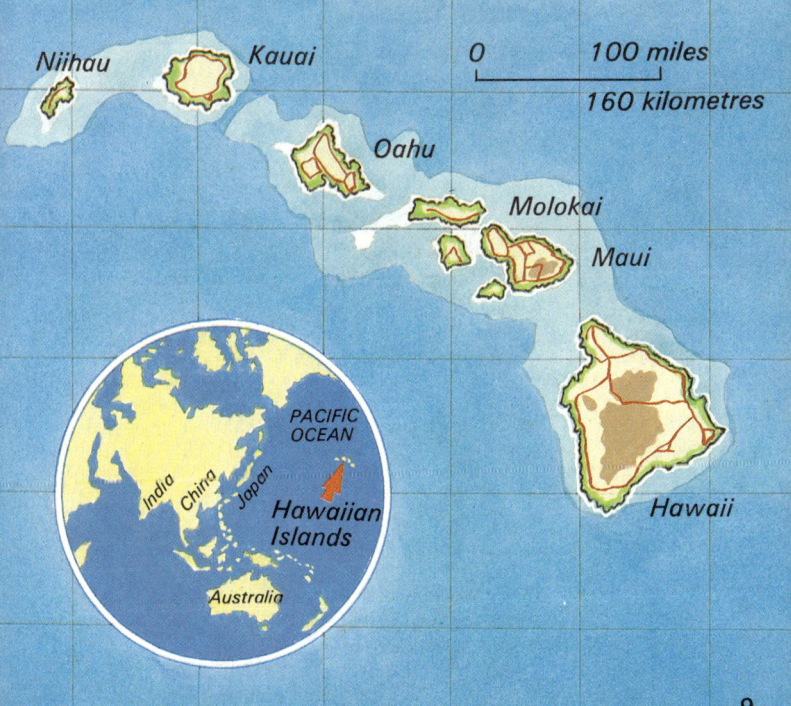

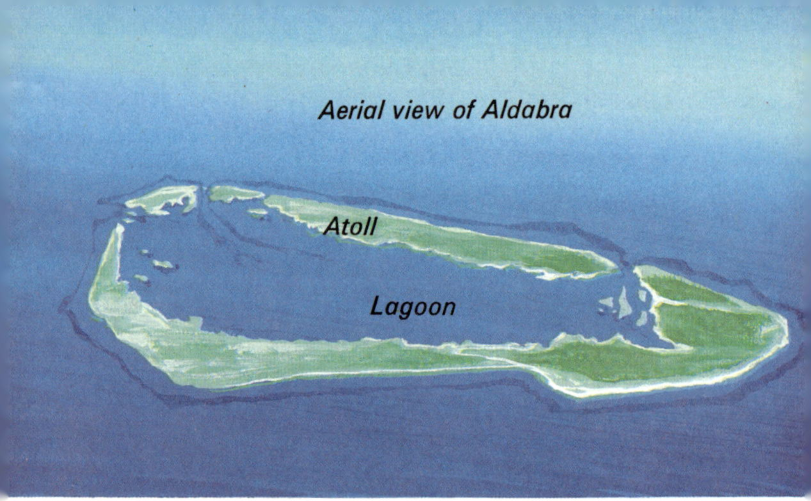

Aerial view of Aldabra

Atoll

Lagoon

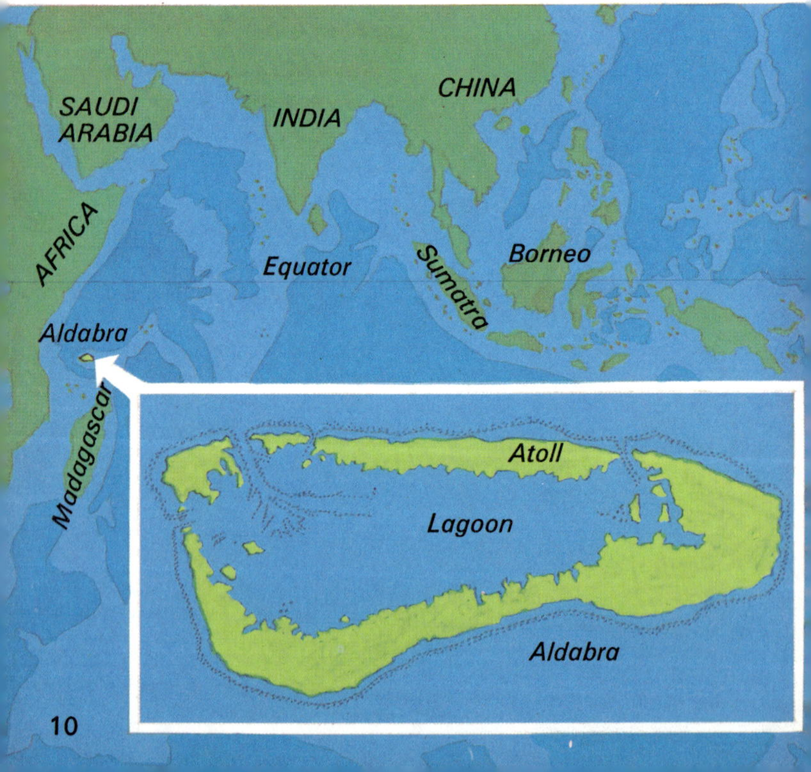

SAUDI ARABIA
AFRICA
INDIA
CHINA
Equator
Sumatra
Borneo
Aldabra
Madagascar

Atoll
Lagoon
Aldabra

Large Fungus Coral

Coral islands

Coral islands form
as the result of the growth
of creatures called coral *polyps*.

These small animals live
in warm shallow seas.

They have hard skeletons of lime
that form rock when the polyps die.

Sometimes, over thousands of years
of coral growth, ring-shaped
or horseshoe-shaped islands form.

They are called *atolls*.

Plants and animals

On coral and volcanic islands
far from other land masses,
there are few types of plants
or land animals.

Some small insects and seeds
may have been blown to an island
by the wind.

Coconuts can float on the sea
for some time
and may grow into trees
when thrown up onto an island
by the waves.

An island explodes

Scientists were able to study
the time it took for plants
and animals to come back
to the island of Krakatoa
after the volcanic explosion of 1883.

Everything on the island
was killed by the eruption.

By 1908 there were 13 kinds of birds and 115 types of plants living on the island.

By 1933 there were 30 kinds of birds and 271 types of plants.

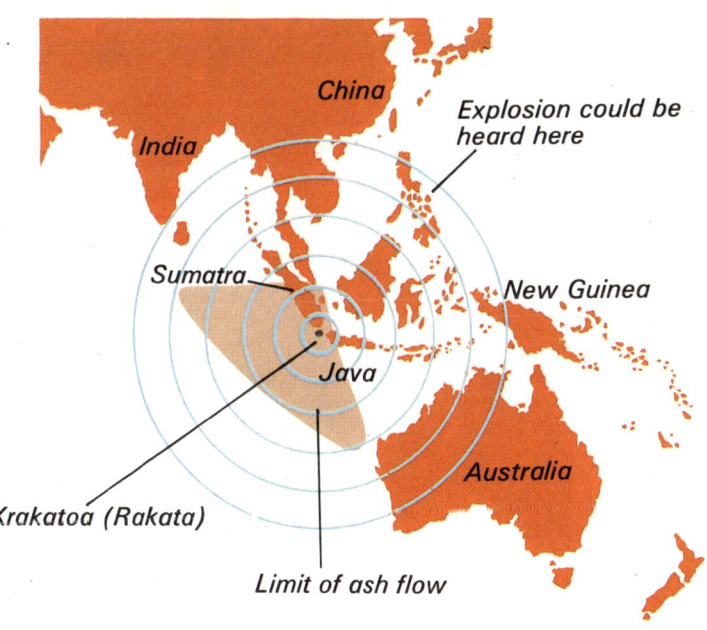

Each ring represents 590 kilometres

Penguin colony

Island sea-bird colonies

Penguins and auks can swim
very well, up to 30 miles (48 km)
an hour.

Other sea-birds such as gulls
and gannets have powerful wings,
and are expert flyers.

They can easily reach islands.

There are few animals
to eat eggs or chicks
so many sea-birds nest on islands.

Gannet colonies

Bass Rock

Gannets

Many millions of penguins
nest on the islands
of the Southern Ocean.

Several thousand pairs of gannets
breed on the Bass Rock
in the Firth of Forth, Scotland.

Flightless birds

Some land birds that have reached islands
have lost the power of flight.

They cannot leave
their island home.

On Gough Island in the South Atlantic there lives a *Flightless Rail*.

It looks rather like a moorhen.

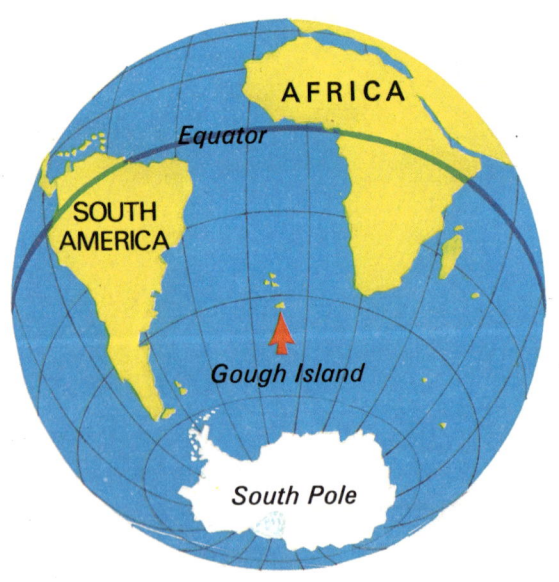

A Flightless Rail

Unique plants and animals

On many islands there are plants and animals that live nowhere else.

The Lundy cabbage is a plant found only on the Isle of Lundy in the Bristol Channel.

Cliffs on the island of St Kilda

On St Kilda in the North Atlantic mice and wrens are found that are different from those elsewhere.

St Kilda Mouse

St Kilda Wren

St Kilda

SCOTLAND

Some strange island creatures

Some of the creatures and plants that live on islands are very strange.

On the Galapagos Islands
in the Pacific there are
tortoises that weigh 225 kilograms,
four-eyed fish,
and cacti that grow like trees.

Comparative size

A Dodo

AFRICA

Dead as the dodo!

For many hundreds of years
seamen have killed for food
birds that lived on islands.

Rats came ashore
from visiting ships and wrecks.

Sometimes cats were left behind.

Cats killed many birds
and other animals.

Rats ate eggs and chicks.

Madagascar

Mauritius

Now many rare creatures,
like the dodo
that once lived on Mauritius,
are *extinct* (there are none left).

Island reserves

Now some islands have been protected as nature reserves so that their scenery and rare plants and animals may be preserved.

No animals are killed and there is no mining or timber cutting on these islands.

Pandanus fruit

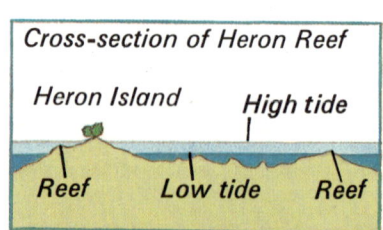

Muttonbird

Giant tortoises

Heron Island off the coast
of Australia and some islands
of the Seychelles
are protected in this way.

Island travel

People often travel to islands by boat.
Some islands only have mail and goods brought by boat once or twice each year.

*Tristan da Cunha
(Sometimes called the
loneliest island in the world)*

Another way of reaching islands
is by aircraft.
Helicopters are sometimes used.
This one flies from Penzance
in Cornwall, England
to the Isles of Scilly.

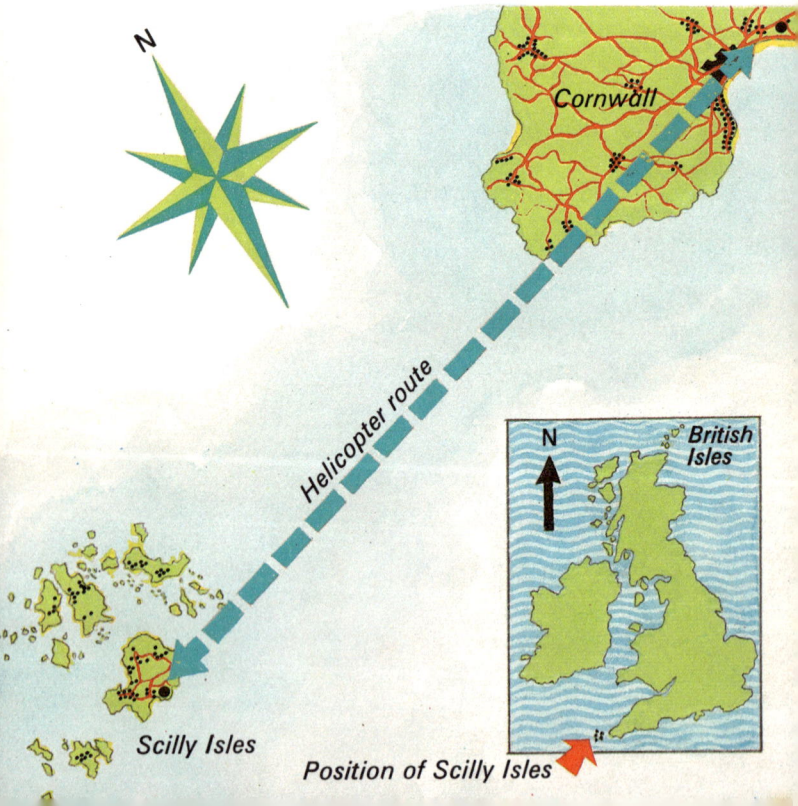

Fishing

Because they have water
all around them,
some island dwellers are fishermen.
They may eat the fish themselves
or sell it.

If it is to be sold
it will probably have to be
frozen, dried or canned.

Farming

Where crops can be grown
and animals kept
some islanders are farmers.

On some islands in the Pacific
pigs are kept.

On islands in the tropics
such as Mauritius
sugar-cane and coconuts
are grown.

Tourism

Many people travel to islands for their holidays.

They enjoy fishing, boating and exploring.

Hundreds of thousands of people
each year travel from England
to Minorca and Majorca
and other Mediterranean islands.

Communications

Some islands are used by jet aircraft needing to refuel on long flights. Thus flights between Australia and Africa stop at Mauritius.

A few islands, like Tonga Island, have cable and radio stations which use satellites to pass messages.

Lighthouses

Some islands are surrounded
by dangerous rocks.
Ships have to be warned
to keep clear,
so lighthouses have been built
as a warning.

*Isle of Shoals Lighthouse 8 km
off New Hampshire, on the East
coast of N. America, north of New York*

An island mystery

Easter Island is
a small volcanic island
in the Pacific Ocean
3200 kilometres
from South America.

On it are many strange statues.

They are 5-6 metres high
and weigh up to 50 tonnes.

They were cut without metal tools
hundreds of years ago.

Nobody knows why they were made
or how they were dragged
to where they stand.

A beautiful island

Bali is a small island in Indonesia famous for its beautiful lakes, volcanoes and beaches.

There are 20,000 temples on Bali's 5,500 square kilometres.

Many people from Australia go to Bali for their holidays.

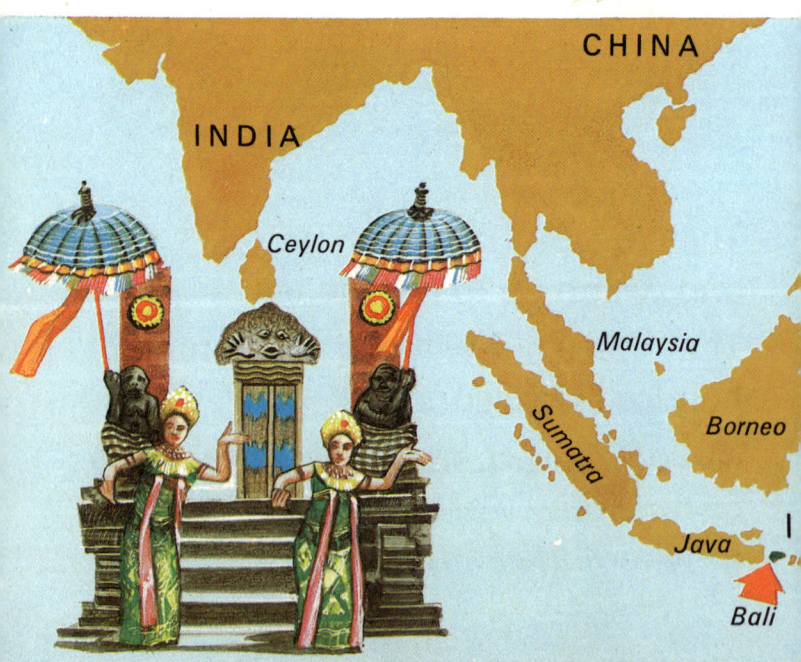

Mont-St-Michel

Some islands can be reached by causeways.

These roads are sometimes covered by water at high tide.

Mont-St-Michel was linked to northern France by a causeway in 1881.

This small islet is the site
of an ancient monastery.

Before the road was built
people crossed to the island
by picking their way
between quicksands.

Rathlin

Rathlin is an L-shaped island
off the north coast of Ireland.

It has steep black and white cliffs.

It was in a cave on Rathlin Island
that Robert the Bruce
is said to have seen
a spider climb up a web
after falling several times.

This encouraged him
to return to Scotland
to fight his enemies once more.

The British Isles

Two large islands and several hundred small ones make up the British Isles.

Shetland Islands
Orkney Islands
Fair Isle
Outer Hebrides
Isle of Skye
Rhum
Mull
Islay
Rathlin Is.
Arran
Holy Island
IRELAND
Aran Is.
Isle of Man
Anglesey
Isles of Scilly
Isle of Wight

Some of the world's islands

1	Baffin Island	11	Gough Island
2	Bali	12	Hawaii
3	Borneo	13	Hebrides
4	British Isles	14	Heron Island
5	Celebes	15	Java
6	Devon Island	16	Kauai
7	Easter Island	17	Lundy Island
8	Ellesmere Island	18	Madagascar
9	Fair Isle	19	Majorca
10	Galapagos Islands	20	Marshall Islands

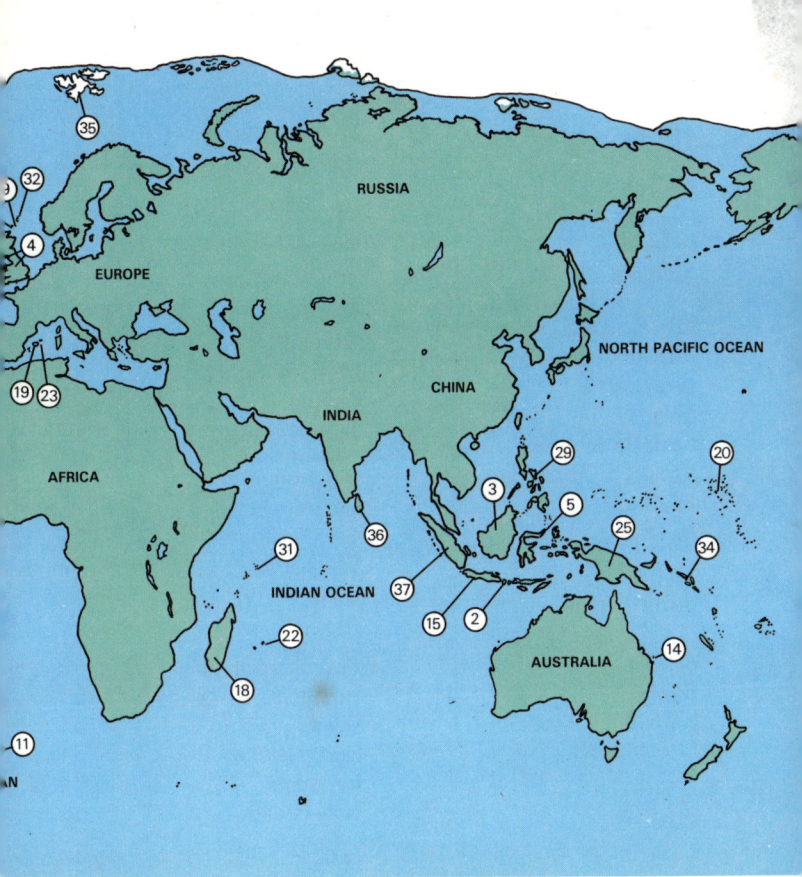

21	Maui	31	Seychelles
22	Mauritius	32	Shetland Islands
23	Minorca	33	Skye
24	Molokai	34	Solomon Islands
25	New Guinea	35	Spitzbergen
26	Niihau	36	Sri Lanka
27	Oahu	37	Sumatra
28	Orkney Islands	38	Tonga
29	Philippines	39	Tristan da Cunha
30	Scilly Isles	40	Victoria Island

Index

	page		*page*
Africa	10, 18, 24, 25, 29, 38	Devon Island	4, 50-51
		Dodo	24, 25
Aircraft	30, 31, 38		
Aldabra	10	Easter Island	42-43, 50-51
Anglesey	49	Ellesmere Island	4, 50-51
Animals	12, 14, 20-24, 26, 35	Europe	6, 7, 29, 38
Antarctica	16, 18	Fair Isle	49, 50-51
Arabia	10	Farming	34-35
Aran Island	49	Fish, four-eyed	23
Arran	49	Fishing	32-33, 36
Atlantic ocean	29	Flightless birds	16-19
Atoll	endpaper, 10, 11		
Auks	16	Galapagos Islands	23, 50-51
Australia	4, 5, 9, 15, 26, 27, 29, 38, 44	Gannets	16, 17
		Gough Island	18, 50-51
		Greenland	4, 29
Baffin Island	4, 50-51	Gulls	16
Bali	44-45, 50-51		
Birds	15-21, 24, 25	Hawaii	9, 50-51
Boats	28, 32-33, 36-37	Hawaiian Islands	9
Borneo	5, 10, 44, 50-51	Hebrides	49, 50-51
British Isles	6, 7, 17, 20, 21, 30, 31, 49-51	Helicopters	30, 31
		Heron Island	26, 27, 50-51
		Holidays	36-37, 44
Celebes	5, 50-51	Holy Island	49
Ceylon (*see* Sri Lanka)			
China	9, 10, 15, 25, 44	India	9, 10, 15, 29, 44
Coconuts	12-13, 35	Indian Ocean	29
Communications	28-31, 38, 39	Indonesia	14, 15, 44
		Insects	12
Coral	11	Ireland	4, 6, 7, 48, 49, 50-51
Coral islands	endpaper, 10, 11, 12	Islay	49
Cornwall	30	Japan	9
Crops	35	Java	5, 15, 44, 50-51